The Kids' Career Library™

A Day in the Life of a
Professional
Golfer

Liza N. Burby

The Rosen Publishing Group's
PowerKids Press™
New York

Special thanks to June C. Staton of the Cedarbrook Golf Club in Old Brookville for her help with this book.

Published in 1999 by The Rosen Publishing Group, Inc.
29 East 21st Street, New York, NY 10010

First Edition

Book Design: Erin McKenna

Photo Illustrations: All photos by Christine Innamorato

Burby, Liza N.
      A day in the life of a professional golfer / by Liza N. Burby.
          p. cm. — (The kids' career library)
      Includes index.
      Summary: Follows a professional golfer through her daily activities as she instructs a student, talks to players at a country club, and prepares for a tournament.
      ISBN 0-8239-5299-1
      1. Golf—Juvenile literature. [1. Golfers. 2. Occupations.]
      I. Title. II. Series.
      GV968.B87 1998
      796.352'023'73—dc21
                                                                    98-5643
                                                                      CIP
                                                                      AC

Manufactured in the United States of America

Contents

Player and Teacher

June C. Staton has been playing golf since she was eight years old. She loves golf. One of the things she likes to do is play in golf **tournaments** (TOR-nuh-ments). Sometimes she wins. Sometimes she loses. But she always has fun playing the game. One day June decided to make a **career** (kuh-REER) of playing golf. June was one of the first female golf **professionals** (proh-FEH-shuh-nulz) in the country. As a professional golfer, she plays golf a lot. And she teaches other people how to play the game too. But that's not all she does!

◄ June C. Staton made it possible for other female golfers to become professionals.

Play Clothes

When June is going to play golf or give a lesson, she makes sure she wears **comfortable** (KUMF-ter-bul), loose-fitting clothes, such as pants and a sweater. Tight clothes would make it hard for June to swing a golf **club** (KLUB). Whatever she wears, it must meet the country club's **dress code** (DRES COHD). June also wears shoes with rubber teeth on the bottom called soft spikes. These spikes grip the ground so that she doesn't lose her balance as she hits a golf ball.

Because players twist and turn a lot when they swing a golf club, it's important to wear loose clothes. ▶

The Lesson Begins

Today June is taking a student onto the **fairway** (FAYR-way) for a lesson. The fairway is the part of the golf course from which it is easiest for people to play golf. June and her student climb into a golf cart. With a flick of the switch, they're off. Riding in a golf cart is fun. When they get to the **tee** (TEE), June reminds her student how to stand as she swings the golf club. June says that in golf, every move a player makes is important.

◀ When playing golf, players can drive in a cart or walk the course.

9

A Game That Is Just Right

June draws a line on the grass with white chalk. This helps her student hit the ball straight ahead. June also reminds her student how to hold the club and where to put her feet. June checks to make sure her student's clubs are the right length for her. This will help her play better. Safety is important too. You have to be very careful not to stand too close to someone who is swinging a golf club. If you do, you could get hit.

As a student practices her swing, June ▶
watches from a safe distance.

Swoop, Thwack!

June takes a turn too. She chooses a club from the bag and gets ready to swing. She looks ahead to see where the ball should go. Then—swoop! Thwack! She hits the ball. She swings so fast that the club digs up some grass and dirt. This is called a **divot** (DIH-vit). The ball soars and disappears. Did it land in the hole? June will check later. She's been playing golf for so long that she can usually tell how close the ball got to the hole without looking. June finds the divot. Then she puts it back where it belongs so that the fairway doesn't get ruined.

◀ While she's swinging a golf club, June keeps her eyes on the ball.

Being Polite

June's student asks her, "Do you have my sand wedge?" A sand wedge is a kind of club that is used to hit a ball out of a **bunker** (BUN-ker), or sand trap. June hands her the sand wedge, and her student hits the ball out of the trap. When they are done, June takes a rake from the cart and rakes the sand trap. She makes the sand smooth for the next player. "Being polite to other players is an important part of playing golf," she says.

It's often hard to hit a ball out of a sand trap. Raking the trap makes it easier for other ▶ players to hit their balls out.

Head Pro

June is the head pro at this country club. That means she is in charge. When she is not teaching, June says, she does a million other things. She likes to go out on the green and talk to the players. The green is the smooth, very short grass at the end of the fairway where the hole is.

"Hello! How's your game?" June asks one of the players. He says he is having fun. She explains some rules to him and answers questions about a tournament he will be playing in soon.

◀ A big part of being the head golf pro at a country club is getting to know the players and talking to them.

A Million Things

June spends a lot of time in the pro shop. The pro shop is where golfers can buy things, such as golf clubs, golf clothes, and golf shoes. She orders all the clothes and shoes that are sold in the shop. June also repairs golf clubs. She pulls out members' golf bags if she knows they are coming to play that day. June even washes the golf carts when they get dirty. She certainly does do a million things! Her dog, Lucy, often keeps her company.

June also spends time planning upcoming ▶
tournaments at the country club.

A Popular Sport

It is not easy to become a professional golfer. You have to be a very good golfer. You also have to take a test that shows you know a lot about the game. You even have to know how to fix a golf cart and how to make a golf shoe! June says it takes a lot of **dedication** (DEH-dih-KAY-shun) to be a golf pro. She works seven days a week, twelve hours a day, even on holidays. Golf is such a popular sport that there are people out on the course almost every day of the year.

◀ All of the things June has learned during her career have made her a great golfer and a great head pro.

Enjoying the Game

Even though she works so hard, June is very happy. She gets to spend her days playing and working at what she loves to do. She has time to herself too. Like Tiger Woods and other professional golfers, June plays in professional tournaments. She takes golf lessons from other golf pros so that she can improve her own game. And she even goes to golf school to learn how to be a better teacher. June says that seeing her students play better is what she likes best about her job. She wants them to enjoy playing golf as much as she does.

Glossary

bunker (BUN-ker) A sand trap on a golf course where the ball can get stuck.

career (kuh-REER) What a person does to earn money.

club (KLUB) A stick with a paddle on the bottom that people use to hit a golf ball.

comfortable (KUMF-ter-bul) Feeling relaxed.

dedication (DEH-dih-KAY-shun) To have a special purpose.

divot (DIH-vit) A piece of grass and dirt that becomes loose when it is struck with a golf club.

dress code (DRES COHD). A set of rules requiring people to wear certain kinds of clothes, such as collared shirts, when playing golf.

fairway (FAYR-way) The closely mowed part of a golf course that is between the tee and the green on each hole.

professional (proh-FEH-shuh-nul) An athlete who gets paid to play a sport.

tee (TEE) The area from which a golf ball is hit at the beginning of play on each hole.

tournament (TOR-nuh-ment) A contest to see who wins the most games.

Index